DK

MATH MADE EASY

4th Grade Workbook

10 Minutes A Day Math

Author Sean McArdle
Consultant Alison Tribley

10-minute challenge

Try to complete the exercises for each topic in 10 minutes or less. Note the time it takes you in the "Time taken" column below.

DK London
Editor Elizabeth Blakemore
Senior Editor Deborah Lock
US Editor Nancy Ellwood
Math Consultants Sean McArdle, Alison Tribley
Managing Editor Christine Stroyan
Managing Art Editor Anna Hall
Senior Production Editor Andy Hilliard
Senior Production Controller Jude Crozier
Jacket Design Development Manager Sophia MTT
Publisher Andrew Macintyre
Associate Publishing Director Liz Wheeler
Art Director Karen Self
Publishing Director Jonathan Metcalf

DK Delhi
Senior Editor Rupa Rao
Senior Art Editor Stuti Tiwari Bhatia
Assistant Editor Nayan Keshan
Art Editors Priyabrata Roy Chowdhury, Anuj Sharma, Aanchal Singal, Priyanka Singh
Managing Editors Soma B. Chowdhury, Kingshuk Ghoshal
Managing Art Editor Govind Mittal
Senior DTP Designer Tarun Sharma
DTP Designers Anita Yadav, Rakesh Kumar, Harish Aggarwal
Senior Jacket Designer Suhita Dharamjit
Jackets Editorial Coordinator Priyanka Sharma

This American Edition, 2020
First American Edition, 2013
Published in the United States by DK Publishing
1450 Broadway, Suite 801, New York, NY 10018

Copyright © 2013, 2020 Dorling Kindersley Limited
DK, a Division of Penguin Random House Company
20 21 22 23 24 10 9 8 7 6 5 4 3 2 1
001–322719–May/2020

A catalog record for this book is available from the Library of Congress.
ISBN 978-0-7440-3113-3

DK books are available at special discounts when purchased in bulk for sales promotions, premiums, fund-raising, or educational use. For details, contact: DK Publishing Special Markets, 1450 Broadway, Suite 801, New York, NY 10018 SpecialSales@dk.com

Printed and bound in Canada

All images © Dorling Kindersley Limited
For further information see: www.dkimages.com

For the curious

www.dk.com

Contents

Time Filler:
In these boxes are some extra challenges to extend your skills. You can do them if you have some time left after finishing the questions. Or these can be stand-alone activities that you can do in 10 minutes.

Place Value

Look carefully to see the position
of each digit from 0–9.

(1) Each of the numbers below has a 5.

Write H if the 5 is in the hundreds position.

Write T if the 5 is in the tens position.

Write O if the 5 is in the ones position.

25 ········· 145 ········· 56 ········· 250 ········· 510 ········· 251 ·········

(2) Which digit is in the hundreds position?

654 ☐   1432 ☐

6,000 ☐   213 ☐

(3) Write the value of the underlined digit.

2<u>5</u> ················   2<u>5</u>0 ··········

<u>2</u>,500 ···············   52<u>0</u> ··········

(4) 26 can be written as 20+6. This is called expanded form. Write each number in its expanded form.

45 ☐

264 ☐

12 ☐

602 ☐

(5) Find the sum.

20 + 8   = ☐

30 + 2   = ☐

100 + 20   = ☐

100 + 10 + 4 = ☐

Time Filler:
Can you figure out what numbers are one more than 2,099 and 3,009? What numbers are one less than 4,000 and 1,050? Can you think of some tricky before and after number challenges for your friends?

6) Mom has saved 10 five-dollar bills towards a vacation. Dad has saved 48 one-dollar coins.

Who has saved the most and by how much?

....

7) Write each of these numbers in expanded form.

2,356 [   ]

4,031 [   ]

1,007 [   ]

3,105 [   ]

8) Find the sum.

$4,000 + 200 + 40 =$ [   ]

$1,000 + 60 + 3 \ =$ [   ]

$6,000 + 400 + 8 =$ [   ]

$1,000 + 1 \qquad =$ [   ]

9) Write the value of the underlined digit.

2,6̲04 [   ]

9,04̲5̲ [   ]

3̲,350 [   ]

4,19̲5 [   ]

10) 40 is the same as 4 tens.

Complete these number sentences.

70 is the same as ....

250 is the same as ....

8 tens are the same as [   ]

17 tens are the same as [   ]

Measuring Length

These questions are all about measuring the length and height of things. Make sure you have a ruler before you start. Use the metric side of the ruler to measure.

1 Which path is longest?

Path A—40 m

Path B—70 m

Path C—43 m

2 How long is each pencil in centimeters (cm)? Use a ruler.

a.

b.

c.

3 Which town is closer to City A and by how much?

Town B

193 km

City A

112 km Town A

4 Which town is closer to City B and by how much?

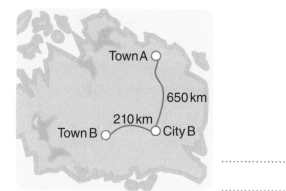

Town A

650 km

210 km

Town B City B

5 What is the height of each pile of bricks in centimeters (cm)? Use a ruler.

a.

b.

c.

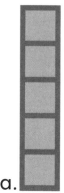
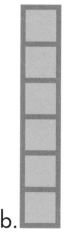

a.   b.   c.

Time Filler:
How many objects can you measure with your ruler in 10 minutes? Choose small ones and larger ones. Make sure you are accurate and always remember to write cm next to the number.

6 Which is the best metric unit to measure each item?

The height of a building ....

The length of an arm ....

The distance between two countries ....

The size of an ant ....

7 Write the answers as meters and centimeters.

60 cm + 90 cm

120 cm + 25 cm

200 cm + 300 cm

8 Which crayon is the longest? Use a ruler.

a.

b.

c.

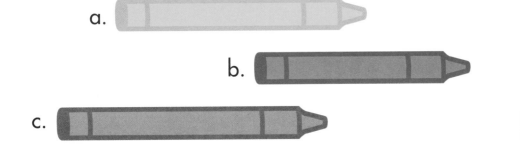

9 If these strips of wood are put end to end, what is their total length?

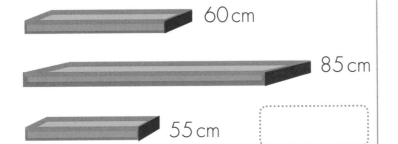

60 cm

85 cm

55 cm

10 Which line is longer and by how much?

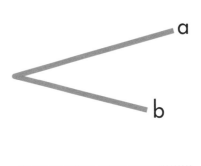

a

b

....

8

2-D Shapes

How well do you know your
2-D shapes? Give these questions a try!

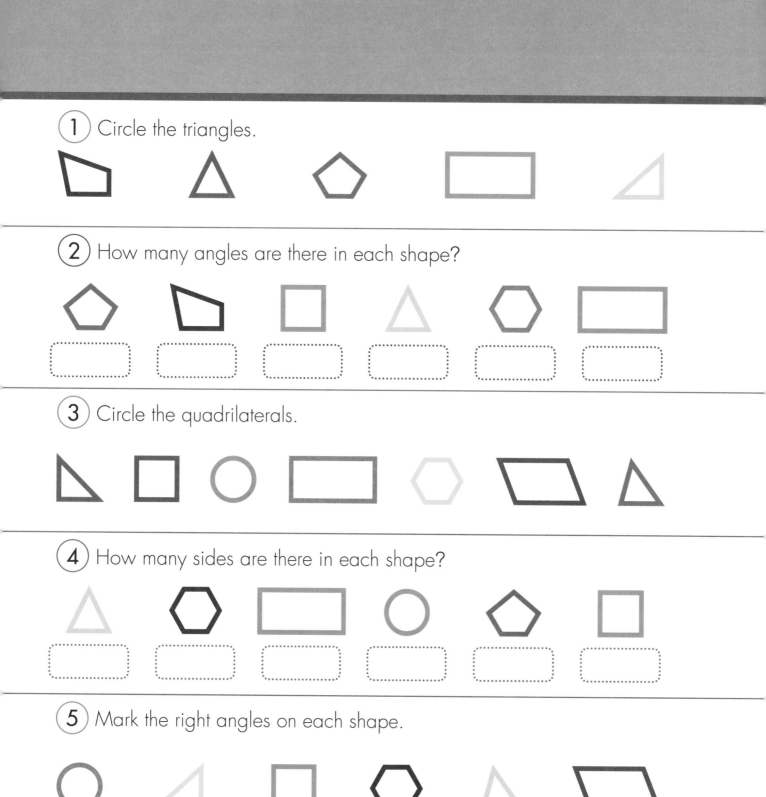

(1) Circle the triangles.

(2) How many angles are there in each shape?

(3) Circle the quadrilaterals.

(4) How many sides are there in each shape?

(5) Mark the right angles on each shape.

Time Filler:
Write some descriptions of shapes just like questions 8 and 10. Can your family and friends guess which shape you are describing?

6) Look at the shapes below and name them.

....

Write one thing the shapes have in common.

....

Write one thing the shapes do not have in common.

....

7) Join the shape name to the correct shape.

Hexagon

Octagon

Pentagon

8) Draw the shape and name it from this description:

The shape has four sides.

The shape has four right angles, one in each corner.

The four sides are the same length. ....

9) Circle the quadrilaterals.

10) Draw the shape and name it from this description:

I have one side.
I have no angles although some people say I have millions. ....

What Comes Next?

Your challenge is to put numbers
in order and to look for the
patterns in these sequences.

(1) Write these rows of numbers in
order with the smallest number first.

7   5   9   2   8

40   70   10   90   50

25   15   5   30   20

(2) Write the next two numbers
in each sequence.

2   4   6   8   ☐ ☐

3   6   9   12   ☐ ☐

5   15   25   35   ☐ ☐

(3) Each day a man doubles the amount of time he exercises.

On Monday, he does 5 minutes.

On Tuesday, he does 10 minutes.

On Wednesday, he does 20 minutes.

How long will he exercise on Thursday and Friday?   ....

(4) Write each row of numbers
in order with the smallest first.

26   18   34   42

53   35   5   3

270   72   27   720

(5) Write the next two numbers
in each sequence.

20   18   16   14   ☐ ☐

60   50   40   30   ☐ ☐

21   18   15   12   ☐ ☐

Time Filler:
Can you write your own sequence with the rule of adding 4 each time? Try spotting the rule in this number sequence: 160, 80, 40, 20, 10, 5. Write some other number sequences to challenge your family.

6) A lady gradually gets better at laying bricks so she doubles the number each hour.
In the first hour, she only lays six bricks.
In the second hour, she lays 12 bricks.
In the third hour, she lays 24 bricks.
How many bricks will she lay in the fourth and fifth hours?

7) Which times table does each row of numbers belong to?

15   18   21   24

21   28   35   42

3   27   33   36

8) Write these amounts in order, starting with the smallest.

75¢   20¢ $1.50   130¢

124 cm   68 cm   1.50 m   0.45 m

90 g   45 g   26 g   48 g

9) A triangle has three sides.
How many sides are there in four triangles?
How many sides are there in six triangles?
How many sides are there in eight triangles?

10) Try to continue this sequence without a calculator.

8   16   32   64

12

Reading Schedules

You do not want to be late for a bus or miss a movie, so try reading these schedules.

Look at this table and then answer the questions.

This is part of a bus schedule.

Greenstar Bus Service—weekdays (AM)					
South Shore	9:05	9:25	9:45	10:05	10:25
Stony Island	9:13	9:33	9:53	10:13	10:33
Lake Park	9:23	9:43	10:03	10:23	10:43
Columbus	9:28	9:48	10:08	10:28	10:48
Wacker	9:43	10:03	10:23	10:43	11:03

1) What time does the 9:05 from South Shore arrive at Wacker?

How long does the journey take?

2) Which two consecutive places are closest by travel time?

Which two consecutive places are farthest apart by travel time?

3) How long is the journey between South Shore and Lake Park?

How long is the journey between Stony Island and Columbus?

4) If I wanted to travel from South Shore to Wacker and arrive in Wacker just before 11:00, which would be the best bus to catch from South Shore?

5) How long is the gap between buses at Lake Park?

Time Filler:
Write your own schedule starting from the moment you wake up on a school day to arriving at school. Put in the approximate time taken for each activity.

This chart shows starting times for movies.

Movies	Start times (PM unless shown)			
Class Wars	1:05	3:20	5:45	8:00
Queen Kong	1:15	3:50	6:00	8:45
Penguins of the Caribbean	11:00 AM	1:15	3:15	5:00
Harry Putter and the Golf Club Mystery	1:30	4:00	6:30	9:00

6) Only one film begins in the morning. Which one?

....

7) Which film begins at 3:50? ....

Which film begins at 6:30? ....

8) If Eli just misses the start of Queen Kong at 3:50, how long will he have to wait for the start of the next showing? ....

9) Which two films have their last showing after 8:30?

....

....

10) Which film begins at 5 o'clock? ....

Which film begins at 6 o'clock? ....

14

Adding Challenge

How quickly and accurately
can you answer these addition
questions? Get set, go!

1 Clara has 27 CDs and
Sandy has 32 CDs.

How many CDs do
they have in total?

2 Oliver has 25 play bricks.
Katie has 18 play bricks.
David has 12 play bricks.

How many play bricks do
they have altogether?

3 a. 42
       + 18

   b. 30
       + 20

   c. 29
       + 11

What do you notice about the three answers?

4 Hasan watches 640 hours of TV in one year.
Nadia watches 480 hours of TV in the same year.

How many hours of TV have they watched in total?

5 a. 200
       + 150

   b. 120
       + 230

   c. 180
       + 170

What do you notice about the three answers?

Time Filler:
How many 3-digit numbers can you make from the digits 1, 2, and 3? Now add three of these numbers together. Try doing the same with the digits 1, 3, and 4.

(6) Peter counts the number of his model cars; he has 57.

Mary does the same thing and finds she has 15 more cars than Peter.

How many cars does Mary have?

(7) a. 67
     + 44

    ....

b. 49
    + 73

    ....

c. 83
    + 29

    ....

(8) Angela is taking a long train trip.

On Day 1, Angela's train travels 176 km.

On Day 2, Angela's train travels 156 km.

On Day 3, Angela's train travels 188 km.

How far has Angela traveled in the three days?

(9) a. 217
     + 97

    ....

b. 489
    + 285

    ....

c. 505
    + 418

    ....

(10) Emmie has 670 songs on her mp3 player.

Darius has 165 more songs on his mp3 player.

How many songs does Darius have?

Measuring Weight

Are you ready for some weight measuring problems to solve? Get steady! Go!

(1) John and Janet had these bags of sugar.

18 oz   18 oz   18 oz   30 oz   30 oz

John's sugar   Janet's sugar

How much sugar does each child have?

....

Who has the most sugar and by how much?

....

(2) The candies each weigh three ounces.

Bill   James   Sarah

What is the weight of Bill's candies?

How much more do Sarah's candies weigh than James'?

(3) How much do the potatoes weigh? Answer in lb and oz.

(4) How many ounces are there in one pound?

(5) How many ounces are there in half a pound?

Time Filler:
Find some open packets of food and weigh them on some weighing scales. How much has been used up?

6 A class of nine-year-olds measured their weights. The average weight of the boys was 62.2 lb and the average weight of the girls was 57 lb. Which group has an average lower weight and by how much?

....

7 A small box of Flakey Flakes weighs 12 oz and a large box of Bran Stix weighs 30 oz.

a.   How much heavier is the Bran Stix than the Flakey Flakes?

b.   How much would four boxes of Flakey Flakes weigh?

c.   Would two boxes of Flakey Flakes weigh more or less than one box of Bran Stix? ....

8 Which weighs more?

10 oz   10 oz   ....
Flour   Feathers   ....

Don't be tricked by this question!

9 A full box of soap powder weighs 26 oz.

Half of the powder has been used. How much does the box weigh now?

10 A coconut weighs 3 lb and 4 oz. Show that weight on the scales below. Note: Each mark on the red scales is 2 oz.

Subtraction

Here are some number problems that all involve subtracting. Remember you can use addition to check your answers. Good luck!

1 Jim has 80 computer games. Anya only has 48 games. Mike only has 64 games.

How many fewer games do Anya and Mike have than Jim?

Anya

Mike

2 a. 34
− 18

b. 50
− 24

c. 71
− 69

....

3 a. 200
− 180

b. 300
− 270

c. 400
− 90

....

4 Rida can jump rope 450 times without stopping.

Yasir can jump rope 385 times without stopping.

How many more times does Rida jump rope than Yasir?

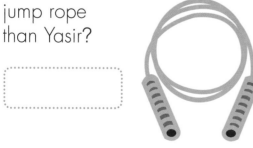

5 After throwing a die 100 times, the number 6 comes up 17 times.

How many times did the other numbers come up?

Time Filler:
Make two numbers from the digits 6, 1, and 5. Then subtract the larger number from the smaller number. Now do the same using the digits 2, 7, and 3. Now change around your numbers. In this way, you can make up your own subtraction questions.

(6) How much more is 250 than 196?

(7) a. 312   b. 431   c. 531
    − 213   − 134   − 315

(8) Bella buys a new cell phone for $164.
    Dante buys the same phone for only $96.
    How much more did Bella pay than Dante?

(9) These are the scores in a basketball game. Which team won and by how many points?

Team H   Team G

118   125

(10) Two numbers add up to 400. One of the numbers is 134. What is the other number?

20

Beat the Clock 1

Test your mental adding and
subtracting skills. How many
can you do in 10 minutes?

(1) 17 + 10 =

(2) 28 – 7 =

(3) 18 + 9 =

(4) 20 – 7 =

(5) 42 – 12 =

(6) 45 – 7 =

(7) 28 + 10 =

(8) 32 – 6 =

(9) 16 + 24 =

(10) 53 + 12 =

(11) 45 – 8 =

(12) 75 + 15 =

(13) 35 + 10 =

(14) 56 – 10 =

(15) 150 + 30 =

(16) 27 + 20 =

(17) 66 – 20 =

(18) 120 – 30 =

(19) 90 + 60 =

(20) 45 – 35 =

(21) 38 + 30 =

(22) 78 – 20 =

(23) 25 + 35 =

(24) 69 – 30 =

(25)
```
   17
 + 13
 ____
```

(26)
```
   14
 + 26
 ____
```

(27)
```
   25
 + 35
 ____
```

(28)
```
   40
 – 19
 ____
```

(29)
```
   56
 + 24
 ____
```

(30)
```
  115
 + 25
 ____
```

Time Filler:
Can you spot the wrong answers
in these number sentences?

$46 + 27 = 73$ $38 - 19 = 29$
$60 - 26 = 44$ $31 + 29 = 70$

Write some questions for your friends
to try. Can they find the wrong ones?

(31) $95 - 40 =$ (32) $47 + 50 =$ (33) $18 - 9 =$

(34) $46 - 40 =$ (35) $8 + 60 =$ (36) $100 - 80 =$

(37) $24 + 24 =$ (38) $120 - 60 =$ (39) $80 + 80 =$

(40) $35 + 35 =$ (41) $53 - 52 =$ (42) $70 + 70 =$

(43) $68 - 66 =$ (44) $43 - 23 =$ (45) $26 - 26 =$

(46) $45 + 45 =$ (47) $54 + 17 =$ (48) $26 + 34 =$

(49) $\begin{array}{r} 29 \\ -19 \\ \hline \end{array}$ (50) $\begin{array}{r} 54 \\ -12 \\ \hline \end{array}$ (51) $\begin{array}{r} 64 \\ -55 \\ \hline \end{array}$ (52) $\begin{array}{r} 42 \\ +18 \\ \hline \end{array}$

(53) $\begin{array}{r} 26 \\ +34 \\ \hline \end{array}$ (54) $\begin{array}{r} 58 \\ -19 \\ \hline \end{array}$ (55) $\begin{array}{r} 37 \\ +13 \\ \hline \end{array}$ (56) $\begin{array}{r} 50 \\ -35 \\ \hline \end{array}$

(57) $\begin{array}{r} 52 \\ +48 \\ \hline \end{array}$ (58) $\begin{array}{r} 48 \\ +12 \\ \hline \end{array}$ (59) $\begin{array}{r} 140 \\ -90 \\ \hline \end{array}$ (60) $\begin{array}{r} 200 \\ +150 \\ \hline \end{array}$

Rounding Numbers

Rounding numbers to the nearest
10, 100, or 1,000 is a useful skill
for estimating answers. Give it a try!

(1) Amir has 48 football posters on his wall.

Rida has 33 pop group posters on her wall.

How many posters does Amir have to the nearest 10?
How many posters does Rida have to the nearest 10?

(2) A box has 49 raisins in it.

To the nearest 10, how many raisins would there be in three boxes?

(3) Marek and Mirka have a race to see who can run the farthest in two minutes.

Marek runs 530 yds and Mirka runs 670 yds.

How far does each child run to the nearest 100 yards?

(4) What is each amount to the nearest 10 ¢?

| 18 ¢ | 27 ¢ | 13 ¢ | 41 ¢ | 65 ¢ |

(5) Igor collects Russian stamps and has 732.

Kira collects stamps from all over the world and has 4,600.

How many stamps does each child have to the nearest 1,000?

Time Filler:
Round each of these amounts to the nearest 10¢: $1.75, 84¢, $3.51, and $2.05. The next time you go shopping, try rounding the amount you have to pay to the nearest 10¢.

6 What is each length to the nearest 100 in?

82 in.   144 in.   370 in.   250 in.   190 in.

7 Most floorboards are about 87 in long.
About how long would three boards placed end to end be to the nearest 10 in?

8 What is each number to the nearest 1,000?

625   4,005   5,612   2,400   7,500

9 If Umi has 78 CDs and Tisa has twice as many, estimate to the nearest 10 how many CDs Tisa has.

10 Diego can swim 6,500 yds without stopping.
Juanita can swim 4,800 yds without stopping.
How far can each swim to the nearest 1,000 yds?

Lines of Symmetry

Is your face symmetrical or do your hairstyle and other features look different on either side of your nose?

1 Draw a line of symmetry on each object.

a.

b.

2 Which shapes do not have a line of symmetry?

a.

b.

c.
....

3 B⊖B has a line of symmetry.

Circle the words that have a line of symmetry.

a. TOT   b. GAG   c. MOM

4 This picture shows half a shape and a line of symmetry. Complete the other half.

5 These shapes have at least two lines of symmetry. Draw all the lines of symmetry you can see.

a.   b.    c.

Time Filler:
Design your own symmetrical pirate face.
Try out a clown face and an animal's
face too, such as a lion or a monkey.

6) Which pirate's face does not have a line of symmetry?

a.    b.    c.    

7) Only two of these letters have
lines of symmetry—which ones?

   a.   T

   b.   S

   c.   Y   ....

8) Complete this face.

9) Draw all the lines of symmetry on these shapes.

a. 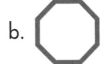   b.    c.

10) Draw lines of symmetry on each number.

   a. **3**   b. **8**   c. **7**

Multiplication Tables

Brush up on your times tables with these questions. Keep them sharp!

1 Carlo has saved 12 nickels. Bella has saved eight nickels. Each nickel is 5¢.

How much money does each child have and who has the most?

....

2 An octopus has eight legs. How many legs does each group have?

3 Darius has two math classes each day.

How many math classes will he have in

5 days? ☐   7 days? ☐   9 days? ☐   11 days? ☐

4 Baseball cards come in packs of six.

How many packs would Salim need to buy to have

30 cards? ☐   18 cards? ☐   48 cards? ☐   72 cards? ☐

5 Marcel puts his comics in piles of three and has 12 piles.
Chantal puts her comics in piles of four and has 11 piles.
Which child has the most comics and by how many?

....

Time Filler:
Can you spot the three times tables
questions that are wrong?

$7 \times 6 = 42$ $6 \times 9 = 53$
$4 \times 5 = 25$ $8 \times 3 = 21$
$3 \times 6 = 18$ $11 \times 6 = 66$

(6) Answer each question.

$2 \times 3 =$ ☐

$3 \times 4 =$ ☐

$4 \times 5 =$ ☐

$5 \times 6 =$ ☐

$6 \times 8 =$ ☐

(7) Otto mixes pink paint by mixing three white cans with one red can.

How many white cans will Otto need if he has seven red cans? ☐

How many white cans will Otto need if he has four red cans? ☐

How many red cans will Otto need if he has 12 white cans? ☐

(8) Ursula saves 5 dollars each week. How many dollars will she have after

four weeks? ☐   seven weeks? ☐   10 weeks? ☐   12 weeks? ☐

(9) How many eights are the same as

16? ☐   24? ☐   40? ☐   56? ☐   88? ☐

(10) Answer each question.

8	10	4	11	6
× 3	× 6	× 5	× 4	× 2

3-D Shapes

How well do you know
your 3-D shapes? Challenge
yourself with these questions.

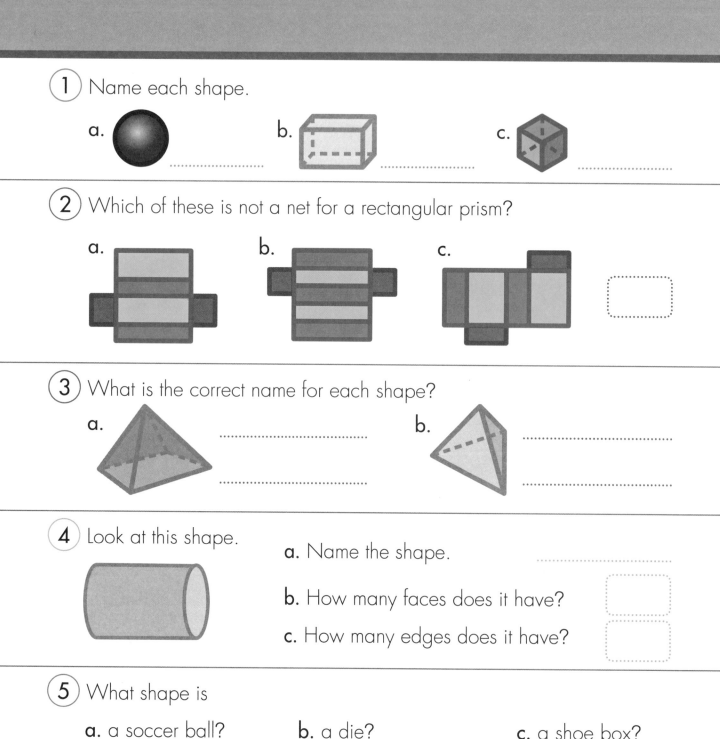

① Name each shape.

a.

b.

c.

② Which of these is not a net for a rectangular prism?

a.

b.

c.

③ What is the correct name for each shape?

a.

b.

④ Look at this shape.

a. Name the shape.

b. How many faces does it have?

c. How many edges does it have?

⑤ What shape is

a. a soccer ball?

b. a die?

c. a shoe box?

Time Filler:
Think of a 3-D shape. How many faces, edges, and vertices (corners) does it have? Can you write three sentences about your shape so that your friends can guess its name?

6 Which of these is not a net for a square-based pyramid?

a.

b.

c.

7 Look at this shape.

a. Name the shape. ....

b. How many faces does it have?

c. How many edges does it have?

8 Complete each sentence.

a. All the faces of a cube are ....

b. A sphere has [ ] curved face(s) and no edges.

9 How many vertices (corners) does each shape have?

a.

b.

c.

10 How many faces does a cube have?

Multiplication

Use your times tables knowledge
to answer these multiplication
questions and solve the problems.

1 In a race, Robert cycles 275 yds. Becky cycles twice as far.

How far does Becky cycle?

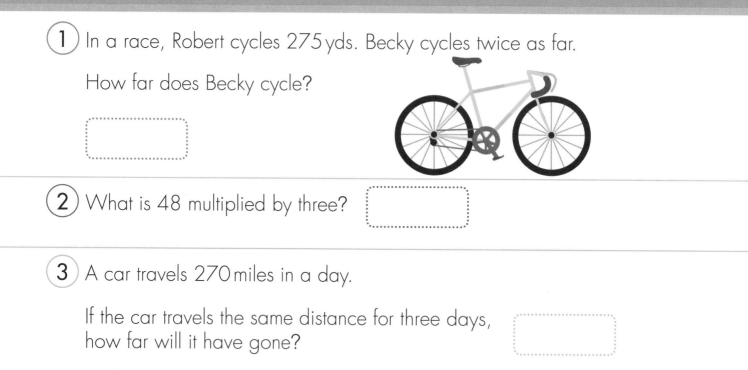

2 What is 48 multiplied by three?

3 A car travels 270 miles in a day.

If the car travels the same distance for three days,
how far will it have gone?

4 Work out each multiplication problem.

a.   72
     x 3
     ....

b.   140
      x 4
      ....

c.   195
      x 2
      ....

5 A gardener grows 16 cabbages in each row.

If the gardener plants six rows, how many cabbages will grow?

Time Filler:
Think of a 3-digit number below 500.
What number is twice as big? What
number is three times as big? Think
of another number and try doing the same.

⑥ Work out each multiplication problem.

a. 50
   x 4
   ....

b. 75
   x 3
   ....

c. 150
   x 4
   ....

⑦ Wendy saves 45 ¢ each week for six weeks.

How much will Wendy have saved after six weeks?

⑧ Shen has downloaded 53 tracks to his mp3 player.
Zan has downloaded three times as many.

How many tracks has Zan downloaded?

⑨ Work out each multiplication problem.

a. 20
   x 4
   ....

b. 40
   x 5
   ....

c. 60
   x 6
   ....

⑩ How much more is nine times ten than nine times nine?

Charts and Tables

Pictographs are very useful in presenting information so that it can be easily used. How quickly can you find the answers?

1 A child kept a record of the birds she saw in her backyard in one week.

Look at this chart and then answer the questions.

Owls	
Robins	
Sparrows	
Starlings	
Swallows	

a. Which bird did she see the most? How many did she see?

....

b. How many more sparrows did she see than robins?

c. How many birds did she see altogether?

d. Which birds did she see only twice?

....

Time Filler:
Draw your own chart using this information of the number of birds seen in a week:

Sparrows 7   Starlings   5
Robins   2   Owls   0
Swallows   2

Remember to give your chart a title.

2 Four children were asked to complete this table about their favorite activities.

Look carefully at this table and then answer the questions.

Name	Music	Sport	Class
Katie	Pop	Jogging	English
David	Jazz	Hockey	Math
Clara	Disco	Gymnastics	Math
Oliver	Pop	Trampoline	Phys Ed

a. Who said hockey was their favorite sport? ....

b. Who had disco as their favorite music? ....

c. Did any of the children enjoy French class? ....

d. How many different types of music are on the table? [   ]

e. Did Clara and Oliver share any favorites? ....

3 Complete the same table for a few of your family or friends.

Name	Music	Sport	Lesson

Write three of your own questions about your table.

a. ....

b. ....

c. ....

Patterns

What comes next in these
shape and number patterns?
Look carefully.

(1) Complete this pattern.

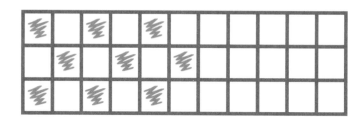

(2) Continue this sequence.

123, 1234, 12345, [   ] [   ]

(3) Continue this pattern.

(4) What comes next?

(5) Fill in the missing numbers.

a. | 0 | 2 | 4 | 6 | | |

b. | 5 | 7 | 9 | | |

Time Filler:
Describe what is happening in each
of these sequences:
3, 9, 27, 81
400, 200, 100, 50
Can you write a sequence with the rule of
multiplying by 2 each time, starting with 4?

(6) Continue this pattern.

(7) Fill in the missing numbers.

a. | 3 | 6 | 9 | 12 | 15 | | | |

b. | 25 | 30 | 35 | 40 | | | |

(8) What comes next?

1,3   2,6   3,9   [ ]   [ ]

(9) Fill in the missing numbers.

a. 49,   42,   [ ]   28,   [ ]   14

b. 63,   54,   [ ]   [ ]   27

(10) What comes next?

Division

Here is a chance to use your times tables knowledge again. This time it is to solve some division problems. Good luck!

1. A pizza is cut into eight slices.

   Four children share the pizza.

   How many pieces does each child receive?

2. 30 bananas are shared equally between five monkeys.

   How many bananas will each monkey receive?

3. Answer each question.

   a. What is 14 divided by 2?

   b. What is 20 divided by 5?

   c. 16 shared by 2 is

   d. 30 shared by 3 is

4. A number divided by 2 is 9.

   What is the number?

5. Answer each question.

   a. $12 \div 2 =$

   b. $15 \div 3 =$

   c. $20 \div 4 =$

   d. $25 \div 5 =$

Time Filler:
A leap year can be divided exactly by 4. Are these leap years: 1886, 1992, and 2024? When will be the next leap year?

6 A farmer gives four hay bales to each cow.

If the farmer gives out 40 hay bales, how many cows does he have?

7 Dave collects 5¢ coins and has saved 50¢.

How many 5¢ coins has Dave collected?

8 Answer each question.

a. What is 35 divided by 5?

b. What is 32 shared by 4?

c. Divide 21 by 3.

d. Divide 45 by 5.

9 Choc Chub candies are put into packs of five.

a. How many packs will be needed for 85 Choc Chubs?

b. How many packs will be needed for 200 Choc Chubs?

10 Four runners run in a relay race.
They each cover an equal distance. The race is 600 yds.

How far does each runner run?

Telling Time

It is time to try some questions about time. How much time will this page take you?

1 Look at this clock.

What will be the time 30 minutes later?

2 Bogdan runs 400 m in two minutes and 30 seconds.

Kamilla runs the same distance in one minute and 50 seconds.

By how many seconds does Kamilla beat Bogdan?

....

3 Circle the months of the year which have 31 days.

January	February	March	April
May	June	July	August
September	October	November	December

4 The clock shows the time Hondo goes to school in the morning.

Show this time on the digital clock.

5 Tisa goes to ballet class at a quarter to four in the afternoon.

Show that time on this clock.

Time Filler:
Can you estimate one minute? Close your eyes. When you think a minute is up, open your eyes. How close were you? Try estimating 2 minutes and 5 minutes. Is it a longer or shorter period of time than you thought?

6 Circle the months of the year which have 30 days.

January	February	March	April
May	June	July	August
September	October	November	December

7 Margaret takes 45 minutes to walk into town.

Roz takes 20 minutes longer than Margaret.

How long does Roz take in hours and minutes?

....

8 This clock is 25 minutes fast.
What is the actual time?

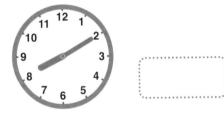

9 Hans begins a race at 10:30 AM.

Hans finishes the race two and a half hours later.

What time does Hans finish the race? Write the time using AM or PM.

10 Put each of these times onto these clock faces:

A quarter to eleven in the morning

Half past six in the evening

Beat the Clock 2

Test your knowledge. How many
questions can you do in 10 minutes?
Get started.

1) $2 \times 3 =$

2) $5 \times 10 =$

3) 1×10

4) $2 \times 5 =$

5) $20 \div 2 =$

6) $20 \div 4 =$

7) $2 \times 10 =$

8) $2 \times 7 =$

9) $3 \times 10 =$

10) $20 \div 5 =$

11) $2 \times 9 =$

12) $10 \times 4 =$

13) $20 \div 10 =$

14) $10 \times 5 =$

15) $3 \times 2 =$

16) $16 \div 2 =$

17) $3 \times 4 =$

18) $10 \times 6 =$

19) $3 \times 6 =$

20) $16 \div 4 =$

21) $3 \times 8 =$

22) $10 \times 7 =$

23) $3 \times 10 =$

24) $8 \times 2 =$

25) $16 \div 8 =$

26) $10 \times 8 =$

27) $2 \times 4 =$

28) $\begin{array}{r} 4 \\ \times 2 \\ \hline \end{array}$

29) $\begin{array}{r} 5 \\ \times 2 \\ \hline \end{array}$

30) $\begin{array}{r} 7 \\ \times 2 \\ \hline \end{array}$

Time Filler:
Multiply 3 by 8, now add 1, now divide by 5, multiply by 6, and divide by 3. What number do you have? Try writing your own questions using multiply, divide, add, and subtract.

(31) 10 x 9 =

(32) 4 x 4 =

(33) 12 ÷ 2 =

(34) 12 ÷ 3 =

(35) 10 x 10 =

(36) 4 x 5 =

(37) 12 ÷ 4 =

(38) 12 ÷ 6 =

(39) 4 x 6 =

(40) 14 ÷ 2 =

(41) 4 x 8 =

(42) 15 ÷ 3 =

(43) 24 ÷ 3 =

(44) 4 x 10 =

(45) 15 ÷ 5 =

(46) 5 x 3 =

(47) 20 ÷ 2 =

(48) 5 x 5 =

(49) 20 ÷ 4 =

(50) 20 ÷ 5 =

(51) 20 ÷ 10 =

(52) 5 x 7 =

(53) 25 ÷ 5 =

(54) 5 x 8 =

(55)   9
     x 2

(56)   3
     x 5

(57)   6
     x 3

(58)   8
     x 4

(59)   6
     x 4

(60) 8)‾40‾ =

Fractions

Get ready to practice fractions.
Here it goes!

(1) Class 3 H has 32 children.

    a. Half the class is girls. How many girls are there in 3 H?

    b. Half the girls have brown hair. How many girls have
    brown hair?

(2) Shade half of each shape.

  a.   **b.**   **c.**

(3) What is half of each number?

  a. 12   **b.** 20   **c.** 8   **d.** 50

(4) Class 4 P has 28 children.

    a. A quarter of the class is home sick.
    How many children are sick?

    b. How many children in 4 P are still
    at school?

(5) Shade one-third of each shape.

  a.   **b.**   **c.**

Time Filler:
Divide each of these numbers by four and multiply by three: 12¢, 40 in, 20 fl oz, and $4.00. Your answers are three-quarters of the amount.

(6) What is a third of each amount?

a. 18¢ [ ]   b. 60 oz [ ]   c. 27 nuts [ ]

(7) Shade three-quarters of each shape.

a.   b.

(8) What is a quarter of each amount?

a. 32¢ [ ]   b. 48 m [ ]   c. $100 [ ]

(9) What is one-fifth of each number?

a. 20 [ ]   b. 50 [ ]   c. 35 [ ]

(10) Rashid has 60¢ a week pocket money and saves three-quarters of it. Pam has 90¢ a week pocket money and saves a third of it.

a. How much does each child save?

b. Who saves more and by how much?

Measuring Volume

Practice calculating volumes of solids and liquids. Remember there are 1,000 milliliters in 1 liter.

1 What amount is shown on this measuring cup?

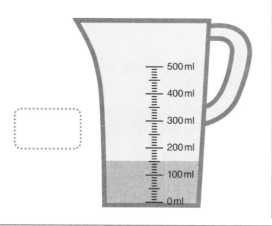

2 a. How many milliliters (ml) are the same as half a liter (l)?

b. How many milliliters (ml) are the same as a quarter of a liter (l)?

3 Label ¼ liter on this measuring cup.

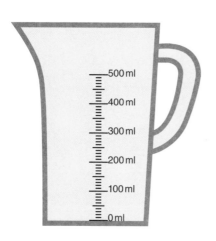

4 Each brick has a volume of 1 cubic centimeter (cm³).

What is the volume of each shape?

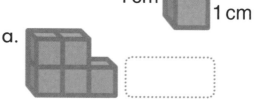

a.

b.

5 Which bucket holds the most water? ....

a. 4 liters   **b.** 9,000 ml   **c.** 6.5 liters

Time Filler:
Find a bowl. How much water can it contain? Use a measuring cup to fill the bowl with water, writing down how much you are pouring in each time. Add your amounts together.

6 Change each amount into milliliters (ml)

a. 6 liters

b. 2.6 liters

c. 1.8 liters

7 How much liquid is there in this tube?

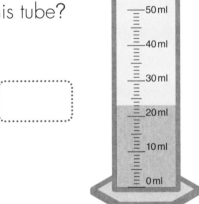

8 Which shape has the larger volume and by how much?

a.

b.

9 Mark the volume 860 ml on this tube.

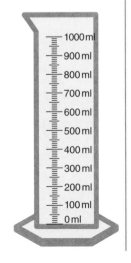

10 Barbara has 0.7 liter (l) of orange juice, Ann has 730 ml, and Harris has 700 ml. Who has the most juice and by how much?

Money Challenge

How quickly can you solve these
questions about money?

① Write these amounts as dollars and cents.

  a. 452 ¢   **b.** 1,270 ¢   **c.** 3,285 ¢

  ....

② Darius has three coins and they add up to 35 ¢.

  What are the three coins?   [ ]   [ ]   [ ]

③ Patrice has these coins in his hand but needs one dollar.

  25 25 25   10   5   1   How much more   [ ]
  TWENTY FIVE C TWENTY FIVE TWENTY FIVE CENTS TEN CENTS FIVE CENTS ONE CENT   does Patrice need?

④ Write these amounts as cents only.

  a. $ 2.36   **b.** $ 7.42   **c.** $ 42.75

  [ ]   [ ]   [ ]

⑤ Bonnie earns 50 ¢ every time she cleans her mother's car.
  How much will Bonnie earn if she cleans the car…

  a. twice?   **b.** 5 times?   **c.** 10 times?

  [ ]   [ ]   [ ]

Time Filler:
Ask an adult for a 25 ¢, a 10 ¢, a 5 ¢, and a 1 ¢ coin. How much do you have? How much more do you need to make $1.00? Ask for three more coins. Do you have enough now?

6 a. How many 25 ¢ have the same value as $1.00?

b. How many 5 ¢ have the same value as $1.00?

c. How many 10 ¢ have the same value as $2.00?

7 Work out each sum.

a. 17 ¢
  + 14 ¢

b. 26 ¢
  + 38 ¢

c. 54 ¢
  + 36 ¢

8 Kareem has three 10 ¢ and two 5 ¢. Salima has two 10 ¢, three 5 ¢, and four 1 ¢.

a. How much does each child have?

b. Who has the most and by how much?

9 Solve the difference.

a. 40 ¢
  − 18 ¢

b. 53 ¢
  − 47 ¢

c. 27 ¢
  − 19 ¢

10 Bella has four coins in her hand. The value of Bella's coins is 41 ¢.
Which coins does Bella have?

Angle Turns

These questions are all about finding and measuring angles. Make sure you have a protractor before you start.

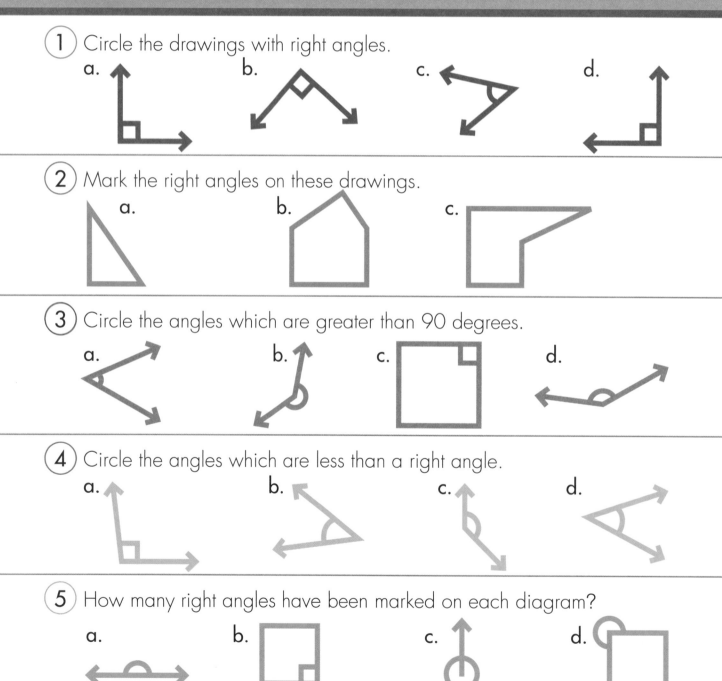

1. Circle the drawings with right angles.
   a.   b.   c.   d.

2. Mark the right angles on these drawings.
   a.   b.   c.

3. Circle the angles which are greater than 90 degrees.
   a.   b.   c.   d.

4. Circle the angles which are less than a right angle.
   a.   b.   c.   d.

5. How many right angles have been marked on each diagram?
   a.   b.   c.   d.

Time Filler:
Draw some 3- or more-sided shapes on a piece of paper using a ruler. First estimate what you think the angles inside each shape might be. Then use a protractor to measure these angles. Were you close?

(6) Use a protractor to measure each angle.

a.

b.

(7) Draw these angles.

a. 40°

b. 65°

(8) Use a protractor to measure each angle.

a.   b.

(9) Draw these angles on the given lines.

a. → 70°   b. → 140°

(10) a. A full turn is the same as [   ] right angles.

b. A three-quarter turn is the same as [   ] right angles.

Problem Solving

Quiet please! Detective at work. Remember to read the question carefully to find out what sort of operation you need to do: +, −, x, or ÷.

1. Jim runs 1,500 yds a day to help him stay fit. How far will Jim have run after

   a. 4 days?   **b.** 6 days?   **c.** 10 days?

2. Ann needs $10.00 to buy presents for her family but only has $8.65. How much more does Ann need?

3. Three children solve the problem: 17 x 3. They each get a different answer.

41	50	51
James	Roisin	Danni

   Who is correct? ....

4. A class of 32 children goes on a picnic. The class needs one carton of milk for every four children.

   How many cartons of milk will they need?

5. Which of these sums is wrong?

   a.   28
          + 19
          —————
           47

   b.   230
          + 170
          —————
           300

   c.   145
          + 125
          —————
           270

Time Filler:
Use a measuring tape to measure the length of your trousers. Now measure the length of your shorts. What is the difference between their lengths?

(6) A teacher buys three coloring pencils for each child in his class. The teacher has 28 children in his class. How many pencils must he buy?

(7) Ben can buy music for his mp3 player at 70 ¢ per song. How many songs can Ben buy with $5? How much will he have left?

(8) Celia's bus is supposed to leave at 10:48 but is 15 minutes late. What time does Celia's bus leave?

(9) Jake fills in a times-table chart but has two wrong answers.

Circle the wrong answers.

	2	3	4	5	8	10
x5	10	15	20	35	40	50
x8	16	22	32	40	64	80

(10) Jonah wants to be as tall as his father. Jonah is 4.56 ft tall. His father is 6.17 ft tall.

How much taller does Jonah need to grow?

Diagrams

Venn diagrams and Carroll diagrams are useful ways of quickly showing comparisons between information.

① Fill in these numbers on the Venn diagram.

4   12   9   14   6   20   27

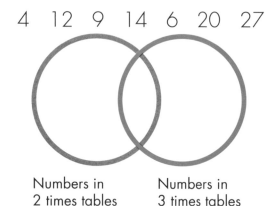

Numbers in 2 times tables   Numbers in 3 times tables

② Look at this Carroll diagram.

Put each item in the correct section—carrot, apple, orange, and cabbage.

	Fruit	Vegetable
Green		
Orange		

③ Label each section of the Venn diagram.

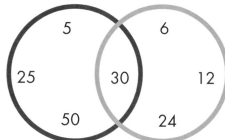

5

25

30

50   24

6

12

....

④ Put each number in the correct section.

14   17   9   4

	Numbers less than 10	Numbers between 11 and 20
Even numbers		
Odd numbers		

⑤ Draw each shape on the Venn diagram.

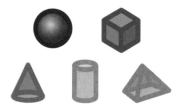

Flat face(s)   Curved face(s)

Time Filler:
Can you think of five numbers that are even and also multiples of 3? Can you think of five numbers that are odd and also multiples of 5?

6. Write each animal name in a section of the Venn diagram— cow, pig, bat, goose, horse, duck, and goat.

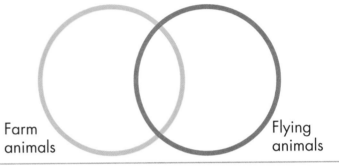

Farm animals

Flying animals

7. Look at this Carroll diagram and then answer the questions.

	Female	Male
Wild	Lioness	Lion
Not Wild	Cow	Bull

a. Which male animal is wild?

....

b. Which female animal is not wild?

....

8. A child says there are no numbers from one to ten that are odd and even at the same time. Show this on a Venn diagram and label the three sections.

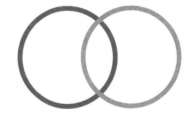

....

9. Two of these people are fictional and two are real. Label this Carroll diagram.

	George Washington	Angelina Jolie
	Harry Potter	Mermaid

10. Label the other two sections of this Venn diagram. Draw in a triangle.

2-D shapes with straight and curved sides

....

Probability Problems

What is the chance of you getting all
these questions correct in 10 minutes?
Feeling confident? Then start!

1. Maggie tosses a penny and it lands with the
   head side up.

   Maggie tosses the coin again. What is the
   probability it will come down heads again?

2. Three cats are in a basket. Two of them are grey and
   one is orange.

   a. What is the probability the orange cat will leave
      the basket first?

   b. What is the probability a grey cat will leave
      the basket first?

3. Daisy rolls a normal six-sided
   die and needs a three to win
   the game.

   a. What is the probability
      Daisy rolls a three?

   b. What is the probability
      Daisy does not roll a three?

4. A school has ten teachers,
   nine women and one man.

   a. What are the chances of
      being in the class with a
      male teacher?

   b. What are the chances of
      having a female teacher?

5. A class has 30 children and two are
   chosen at random to meet a famous TV star.
   What are the chances of being chosen?

Time Filler:
200 people enter a lottery but only
1 in 10 can win a prize. How many
people win a prize? Can you think
of your own probability questions
to test out on your family?

6 A fruit basket has three apples and two oranges.
Peter closes his eyes and picks out one piece of fruit.

   a. What are the chances Peter will pick an apple?

   b. What are the chances Peter will pick an orange?

7 Abi says she is going to swim from England to the U.S.
Circle how possible you think that is.

Certain   Likely   Unlikely   Impossible

8 Don needs to roll 4, 5, or 6 on a normal die to win a game.
What are the chances Don will roll one of those numbers?

9 A teacher has a class of 20 children and has five prizes to
give out at random.
What are the chances of being given a prize?

10 A magician has two white mice and two brown mice in a hat.
The magician asks a child to carefully take one mouse out of the
hat without looking.
What are the chances a white mouse will be taken?

Measuring Speed

Here are some problems to solve about speed. How quickly can you answer them correctly?

(1) Jacek walks 3 miles in one hour. Victoria walks 4 miles in two hours.

If they continue walking at the same speed, how far will they each walk in 6 hours?

....

(2) Krysta cycles 0.2 miles in 3 minutes.

a. If Krysta cycles at the same speed, how long will it take her to cycle 1 mile?

....

b. What speed is Krysta cycling in miles per hour?

....

(3) Marcel swims 1,200 yds in half an hour.
Angelique swims 500 yds in 15 minutes.
After one hour, who has swam the farthest and by what distance?

....

(4) A car travels at 60 mph for one hour.
How far does it travel every ten minutes?

....

(5) A tortoise can travel 8 in in ten minutes.

If the tortoise keeps the same speed, how far will it travel in two hours?

....

Time Filler:
Measure out a distance of 10 yards. How many laps up and down can you do in 1 minute? If you kept running at the same speed for 1 hour, how many laps could you do? (Hint: x60)

6) Billy drives his car at the same speed for three hours. In three hours, Billy travels 180 miles.

What is Billy's speed?

7) A train can go from New York City to Trenton in 60 minutes. The distance for the train is 60 miles.

A car travels the same distance but in 90 minutes.

What is the speed of the car?

8) Daisy jogs a distance of 2 miles in 20 minutes.

a. If Daisy jogs at the same speed all the time, how far can she jog in one hour?

b. How far does Daisy jog in one minute?

9) Which is fastest?

a. 200 yds traveled in 5 minutes.

b. 300 yds traveled in 15 minutes.

c. 400 yds traveled in 20 minutes.

10) Katie's bus travels at a steady speed of 60 miles per hour. The bus travels 240 miles. How long has Katie been traveling?

Tables and Charts

Remember, counting in fives is a common way of quickly counting up tallies.

Tommy collects information about the different types of birds in his garden. He collects the data using a tally chart. These are his results.

Birds	Tallies
Sparrow	卌 卌 卌 卌 卌 IIII
Robin	卌 III
Hummingbird	I
Cardinal	IIII
Blue Jay	卌 卌 卌 卌 II
Pigeon	卌 卌 卌 III

1) a. How many robins did Tommy see?

   b. How many pigeons did Tommy see?

2) a. Which bird did Tommy see the most?

   b. Which bird did Tommy see the least?

3) How many birds did Tommy see in total?

4) How many more sparrows did Tommy see than blue jays?

5) How many types of bird did Tommy see less than ten times?

Time Filler:
Write these numbers as tally marks: 4, 18, 30, and 13. Make a tally chart of how many of each type of clothing you have.

A group of friends make a chart of their classmates' favorite sports. Each child could choose just one sport.

These are the results.

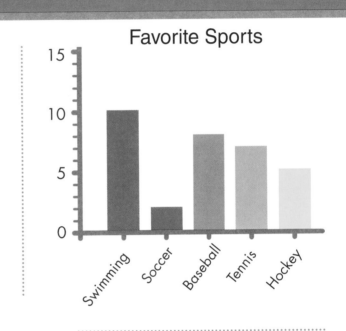

Favorite Sports

6) a. Which was the favorite sport?

b. Which was the least favorite sport?

7) How many more children preferred baseball to tennis?

8) How many children were there in the class?

9) Which two sports together had a total vote of 7?

10) Put a label on each axis.

More Fractions

Equivalent fractions are fractions that have the same value as each other. Remember to multiply or divide the numerator with the same number as the denominator.

1 Circle the fractions that are equivalent to ½.

$\frac{3}{4}$ $\frac{2}{4}$ $\frac{5}{4}$ $\frac{1}{4}$ $\frac{3}{6}$

2 Write two fractions of your own that are equivalent to ½.

3 Half of Megan's socks are red and half are pink. Megan has ten pairs of socks.

What fraction of Megan's socks are red that is equivalent to ½?

4 Circle the fractions that are equivalent to ⅓.

$\frac{2}{6}$ $\frac{3}{6}$ $\frac{4}{10}$ $\frac{3}{9}$ $\frac{4}{8}$

5 Write two fractions of your own that are equivalent to ⅓.

Time Filler:
Draw a circle and color in the fraction ¾.
Now show the color part as the equivalent
fraction ⁶⁄₈ on the circle. Then show as ¹²⁄₁₆
and ³⁰⁄₄₀ by drawing on more lines with a ruler.

6 Write three other fractions that are
equivalent to ⅕.

[ ]   [ ]   [ ]

7 Billy has 12 pennies but gives half away.

Write as a fraction, the number of pennies Billy
gives away that is equivalent to ½.   [ ]

8 Part of these equivalent fractions have been filled
in but parts are missing. Fill in the missing parts.

½ is equivalent to

²⁄? [ ]   ⁴⁄? [ ]   ?⁄10 [ ]   ?⁄20 [ ]

9 Kirk has 20 colored pebbles and gives 5 to Spock.
Kirk says he has given ¼ away. Is he correct?   ....

10 Part of these equivalent fractions have been filled
in but parts are missing. Fill in the missing parts.

⅓ is equivalent to

²⁄? [ ]   ⁴⁄? [ ]   ?⁄12 [ ]   ?⁄30 [ ]

Directions

Compass directions, grid references, and coordinates all help to show the position of things.

(1) Label the three missing points on this 4-point compass.

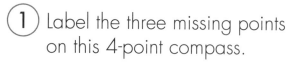

N

(2) What's between Jenny and the dog?

....

(3) Place an X in the square C2.

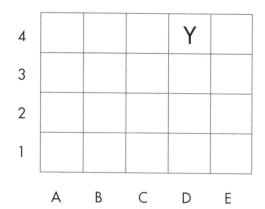

4

3

2

1

A B C D E

(4) On the same grid, what is the position of Y?

....

(5) On the grid in question 3, what is the position of the square halfway between A2 and E2?

....

Time Filler:
Draw a 4 by 4 grid of your own and mark four points with an x. Ask a friend or family member to name the points. Were they correct?

(6) Label the four missing points on this 8-point compass.

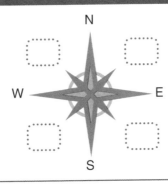

(7) Label the points A (2,1) and B (3,4).

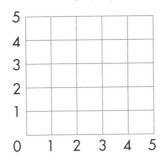

(8) On the grid, what are the coordinates of C and D?

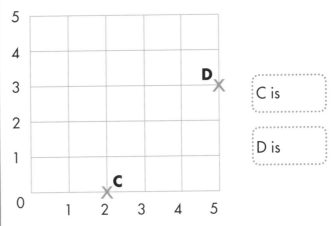

C is

D is

(9) Put these coordinates on the grid and connect them.
(1,1) (1,5) (5,5) (5,1)

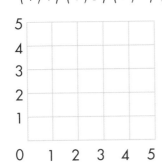

What shape do you have?

(10) What is the coordinate of each point?

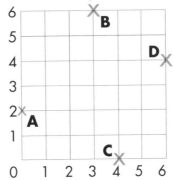

A is

B is

C is

D is

Beat the Clock 3

Can you beat the clock for a third time solving all these 60 mixed-up, mental arithmetic questions in 10 minutes? That is 10 seconds for each one! Get set, go!

1. $1 + 2 + 3 =$

2. Half of 8 =

3. $2 \times 3 =$

4. 12 divided by 2 =

5. $4 + 2 + 1 =$

6. Half of 12 =

7. 5 times six =

8. 16 shared by 2 =

9. $5 + 4 + 3 =$

10. Half of 20 =

11. $9 \times 2 =$

12. $14 \div 2 =$

13. $2 + 2 + 2 + 2 =$

14. Half of 30 =

15. 20 minus 4 =

16. $6 + 8 + 2 =$

17. $30 \div 10 =$

18. Half of 40 =

19. 14 minus 9 =

20. $7 + 6 + 5 =$

21. $40 \div 10 =$

22. Half of 50 =

23. 18 minus 7 =

24. $14 + 2 + 6 =$

25. $100 \div 10 =$

26. $3 + 3 + 3 =$

27. $5 - 5 =$

28. $17 + 12 =$

29. Half of 60 =

30. $4 + 2 + 10 =$

Time Filler:
Think of an even number between 10 and 50, take half of it, add 3, multiply by five, double it, and divide by five. What do you need to subtract to get back to your original number? Try this again with another number.

31) Half of 80 =

32) 42 − 3 =

33) 5 + 5 + 5 =

34) 50 ÷ 10 =

35) 18 − 8 =

36) Half of 100 =

37) Double 5 =

38) 4 + 4 + 2 =

39) 3 x 20 =

40) 100 − 10 =

41) Double 6 =

42) 80 ÷ 8 =

43) 30 x 2 =

44) 70 − 30 =

45) 40 x 2 =

46) 3 sets of 8 =

47) 50 x 2 =

48) 60 − 50 =

49) Double 7 =

50) 6 sets of 5 =

51) 20 x 3 =

52) 6 x 3 =

53) Double 6 =

54) 20 ÷ 4 =

55) 44 − 6 =

56) 6 ÷ 6 =

57) Double 9 =

58) 4 ÷ 4 =

59) Double 10 =

60) 70 − 24 =

66

Answers:

4–5 Place Value
6–7 Measuring Length

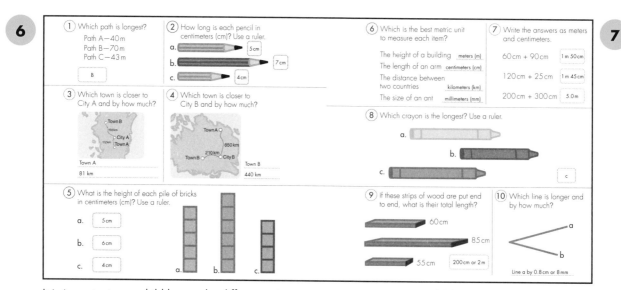

4

① Each of the numbers below has a 5.
Write H if the 5 is in the hundreds position.
Write T if the 5 is in the tens position.
Write O if the 5 is in the ones position.
25 _O_   145 _O_   56 _T_   250 _T_   510 _H_   251 _T_

② Which digit is in the hundreds position?
654 [6]   1432 [4]
6,000 [0]   213 [2]

③ Write the value of the underlined digit.
25 _5 ones_   250 _5 tens_
2,500 _2 thousands_   520 _0 ones_

④ 26 can be written as 20+6. This is called expanded form. Write each number in its expanded form.
45 [40 + 5]
264 [200 + 60 + 4]
12 [10 + 2]
602 [600 + 2]

⑤ Find the sum.
20 + 8 = [28]
30 + 2 = [32]
100 + 20 = [120]
100 +10 + 4 = [114]

⑥ Mom has saved 10 five-dollar bills towards a vacation. Dad has saved 48 one-dollar coins.
Who has saved the most and by how much?
Mom by $2

⑦ Write each of these numbers in expanded form.
2,356 [2,000 + 300 + 50 + 6]
4,031 [4,000 + 30 + 1]
1,007 [1,000 + 7]
3,105 [3,000 + 100 + 5]

⑧ Find the sum.
4,000 + 200 + 40 = [4,240]
1,000 + 60 + 3 = [1,063]
6,000 + 400 + 8 = [6,408]
1,000 + 1 = [1,001]

⑨ Write the value of the underlined digit.
2,604 [6 hundreds]
9,045 [5 ones]
3,350 [3 thousands]
4,195 [9 tens]

⑩ 40 is the same as 4 tens. Complete these number sentences.
70 is the same as [7 tens]   8 tens are the same as [80]
250 is the same as [25 tens]   17 tens are the same as [170]

5

The idea of a child being able to give a value to a digit by its position is fundamental to understanding how numbers and calculations work. Being able to write numbers in the expanded form ex. 17 is 10+7 is vital. Breaking down numbers in this way is also called partitioning.

6

① Which path is longest?
Path A—40m
Path B—70m
Path C—43m
[B]

② How long is each pencil in centimeters (cm)? Use a ruler.
a. [5cm]
b. [7cm]
c. [4cm]

③ Which town is closer to City A and by how much?
Town A
81 km

④ Which town is closer to City B and by how much?
Town B
440 km

⑤ What is the height of each pile of bricks in centimeters (cm)? Use a ruler.
a. [5cm]
b. [6cm]
c. [4cm]

⑥ Which is the best metric unit to measure each item?
The height of a building [meters (m)]
The length of an arm [centimeters (cm)]
The distance between two countries [kilometers (km)]
The size of an ant [millimeters (mm)]

⑦ Write the answers as meters and centimeters.
60 cm + 90 cm [1 m 50 cm]
120 cm + 25 cm [1 m 45 cm]
200 cm + 300 cm [5.0 m]

⑧ Which crayon is the longest? Use a ruler.
[c]

⑨ If these strips of wood are put end to end, what is their total length?
60 cm
85 cm
55 cm
[200cm or 2m]

⑩ Which line is longer and by how much?
Line a by 0.8 cm or 8 mm

7

It is important your child knows the different units in full and abbreviated forms ex. meters and m. At this point, the spelling of the words is not so important as your child's ability to say the word. Many items are given US Customary System measures ex. distance expressed in miles.

Answers:

8–9 2-D Shapes
10–11 What Comes Next?

8

1 Circle the triangles.

2 How many angles are there in each shape?
5 angles | 4 angles | 4 angles | 3 angles | 6 angles | 4 angles

3 Circle the quadrilaterals.

4 How many sides are there in each shape?
3 sides | 6 sides | 4 sides | 1 side | 5 sides | 4 sides

5 Mark the right angles on each shape.

9

6 Look at the shapes below and name them.
Square | Rectangle
Write one thing the shapes have in common.
They each have four right angles. Other answers: They each have 4 sides or 2 parallel sides.
Write one thing the shapes do not have in common.
All sides are not the same length in the rectangle.

7 Join the shape name to the correct shape.
Hexagon
Octagon
Pentagon

8 Draw the shape and name it from this description:
The shape has four sides. The shape has four right angles, one in each corner. The four sides are the same length. Square

9 Circle the quadrilaterals.

10 Draw the shape and name it from this description:
I have one side. I have no angles although some people say I have millions. Circle

Children should be able to recognize and name each shape and describe it accurately and simply. Parents could play a simple "What am I?" game by asking something such as, "I have three sides, three corners, and three angles. What am I?" The game can be developed with details such as the previous example but by adding further, "I have a right angle in one corner."

10

1 Write these rows of numbers in order with the smallest number first.
7 5 9 2 8 → 2 5 7 8 9
40 70 10 90 50 → 10 40 50 70 90
25 15 5 30 20 → 5 15 20 25 30

2 Write the next two numbers in each sequence.
2 4 6 8 10 12
3 6 9 12 15 18
5 15 25 35 45 55

3 Each day a man doubles the amount of time he exercises. On Monday, he does 5 minutes. On Tuesday, he does 10 minutes. On Wednesday, he does 20 minutes. How long will he exercise on Thursday and Friday? 40 minutes on Thursday 80 minutes on Friday

4 Write each row of numbers in order with the smallest first.
26 18 34 42 → 18 26 34 42
53 35 5 3 → 3 5 35 53
270 72 27 720 → 27 72 270 720

5 Write the next two numbers in each sequence.
20 18 16 14 12 10
60 50 40 30 20 10
21 18 15 12 9 6

11

6 A lady gradually gets better at laying bricks so she doubles the number each hour. In the first hour, she only lays six bricks. In the second hour, she lays 12 bricks. In the third hour, she lays 24 bricks. How many bricks will she lay in the fourth and fifth hours? 48 96

7 Which times table does each row of numbers belong to?
15 18 21 24 → 3
21 28 35 42 → 7
3 27 33 36 → 3

8 Write these amounts in order, starting with the smallest.
75¢ 20¢ $1.50 130¢ → 20¢ 75¢ 130¢ $1.50
124cm 68cm 1.50m 0.45m → 0.45m 68cm 124cm 1.50m
90g 45g 26g 48g → 26g 45g 48g 90g

9 A triangle has three sides. How many sides are there in four triangles? 12 How many sides are there in six triangles? 18 How many sides are there in eight triangles? 24

10 Try to continue this sequence without a calculator.
8 16 32 64 128 256

Placing numbers in order is a simple but important skill, which will be used in many ways, including negative numbers at a later stage. Recognizing sequences and being able to continue them is another important skill which can be used in many ways, including algebra.

Answers:

12-13 Reading Schedules
14-15 Adding Challenge

12

Look at this table and then answer the questions.
This is part of a bus schedule.

Greenstar Bus Service—weekdays (AM)					
South Shore	9:05	9:25	9:45	10:05	10:25
Stony Island	9:13	9:33	9:53	10:13	10:33
Lake Park	9:23	9:43	10:03	10:23	10:43
Columbus	9:28	9:48	10:08	10:28	10:48
Wacker	9:43	10:03	10:23	10:43	11:03

(1) What time does the 9:05 from South Shore arrive at Wacker?

9:43

How long does the journey take? 38 minutes

(2) Which two consecutive places are closest by travel time?

Lake Park and Columbus

Which two consecutive places are farthest apart by travel time?

Columbus to Wacker

(3) How long is the journey between South Shore and Lake Park?

18 minutes

How long is the journey between Stony Island and Columbus?

15 minutes

(4) If I wanted to travel from South Shore to Wacker and arrive in Wacker just before 11:00, which would be the best bus to catch from South Shore?

The 10:05 from South Shore.

(5) How long is the gap between buses at Lake Park?

20 minutes

13

This chart shows starting times for movies.

Movies	Start times (PM unless shown)			
Class Wars	1:05	3:20	5:45	8:00
Queen Kong	1:15	3:50	6:00	8:45
Penguins of the Caribbean	11:00 AM	1:15	3:15	5:00
Harry Putter and the Golf Club Mystery	1:30	4:00	6:30	9:00

(6) Only one film begins in the morning. Which one?

Penguins of the Caribbean

(7) Which film begins at 3:50? Queen Kong

Which film begins at 6:30? Harry Putter and the Golf Club Mystery

(8) If Eli just misses the start of Queen Kong at 3:50, how long will he have to wait for the start of the next showing? 2 hours 10 minutes

(9) Which two films have their last showing after 8:30?

Queen Kong

Harry Putter and the Golf Club Mystery

(10) Which film begins at 5 o'clock? Penguins of the Caribbean

Which film begins at 6 o'clock? Queen Kong

Reading from tables and lists is a very useful skill even at an early age. Seeing what time a movie starts or the schedule of buses, for example, can help your child become independent. The questions here can be supported by actual examples taken from your town or city.

14

(1) Clara has 27 CDs and Sandy has 32 CDs.

How many CDs do they have in total?

59

(2) Oliver has 25 play bricks. Katie has 18 play bricks. David has 12 play bricks.

How many play bricks do they have altogether?

55

(3) a.   42
    + 18

     60

b.   30
    + 20

     50

c.   29
    + 11

     40

What do you notice about the three answers?
They each end in zero or are multiples of 10.

(4) Hasan watches 640 hours of TV in one year. Nadia watches 480 hours of TV in the same year.

How many hours of TV have they watched in total? 1,120 hours

(5) a.   200
    + 150

     350

b.   120
    + 230

     350

c.   180
    + 170

     350

What do you notice about the three answers?
The answers are the same.

15

(6) Peter counts the number of his model cars; he has 57.
Mary does the same thing and finds she has 15 more cars than Peter.

How many cars does Mary have? 72

(7) a.   67
    + 44

     111

b.   49
    + 73

     122

c.   83
    + 29

     112

(8) Angela is taking a long train trip.
On Day 1, Angela's train travels 176 km.
On Day 2, Angela's train travels 156 km.
On Day 3, Angela's train travels 188 km.
How far has Angela traveled in the three days? 520 km

(9) a.   217
    + 97

     314

b.   489
    + 285

     774

c.   505
    + 418

     923

(10) Emmie has 670 songs on her mp3 player.
Darius has 165 more songs on his mp3 player.

How many songs does Darius have? 835

Although these questions are fairly basic, children will recognize different ways of using the addition operation. Phrases such as "what is the total" and "put together" need to be recognized and reinforced.

Answers:

16–17 Measuring Weight
18–19 Subtraction

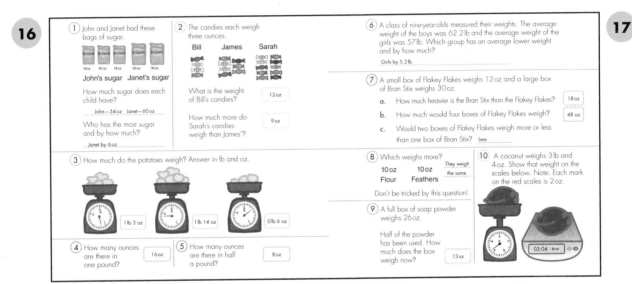

16

① John and Janet had these bags of sugar.

John's sugar   Janet's sugar

How much sugar does each child have?

John—54 oz   Janet—60 oz

Who has the most sugar and by how much?

Janet by 6 oz

② The candies each weigh three ounces.

Bill   James   Sarah

What is the weight of Bill's candies?   12 oz

How much more do Sarah's candies weigh than James'?   9 oz

③ How much do the potatoes weigh? Answer in lb and oz.

1 lb 3 oz   1 lb 14 oz   0 lb 6 oz

④ How many ounces are there in one pound?   16 oz

⑤ How many ounces are there in half a pound?   8 oz

17

⑥ A class of nine-year-olds measured their weights. The average weight of the boys was 62.2 lb and the average weight of the girls was 57 lb. Which group has an average lower weight and by how much?

Girls by 5.2 lb

⑦ A small box of Flakey Flakes weighs 12 oz and a large box of Bran Stix weighs 30 oz.
a. How much heavier is the Bran Stix than the Flakey Flakes?   18 oz
b. How much would four boxes of Flakey Flakes weigh?   48 oz
c. Would two boxes of Flakey Flakes weigh more or less than one box of Bran Stix?   Less

⑧ Which weighs more?
10 oz   10 oz   They weigh the same.
Flour   Feathers
Don't be tricked by this question!

⑨ A full box of soap powder weighs 26 oz.
Half of the powder has been used. How much does the box weigh now?   13 oz

⑩ A coconut weighs 3 lb and 4 oz. Show that weight on the scales below. Note: Each mark on the red scales is 2 oz.

A basic knowledge of the inter-relationship between units is important ex. 16 oz = 1 lb. Practical use of weighing scales is very helpful as scale types vary hugely with both analogue and digital types. Question 8 is a trick but raises important questions about mass and weight for a younger child—are they the same?

18

① Jim has 80 computer games. Anya only has 48 games. Mike only has 64 games.

How many fewer games do Anya and Mike have than Jim?

Anya   **Mike**
Anya—32   Mike—16

② a. 34
      − 18
      16

b. 50
   − 24
   26

c. 71
   − 69
   2

③ a. 200
      − 180
      20

b. 300
   − 270
   30

c. 400
   − 90
   310

④ Rida can jump rope 450 times without stopping.
Yasir can jump rope 385 times without stopping.
How many more times does Rida jump rope than Yasir?   65

⑤ After throwing a die 100 times, the number 6 comes up 17 times.
How many times did the other numbers come up?   83

19

⑥ How much more is 250 than 196?   54

⑦ a. 312
      − 213
      99

b. 431
   − 134
   297

c. 531
   − 315
   216

⑧ Bella buys a new cell phone for $164. Dante buys the same phone for only $96. How much more did Bella pay than Dante? $68

⑨ These are the scores in a basketball game. Which team won and by how many points?

Team H   **Team G**
118   125   Team G by 7 points

⑩ Two numbers add up to 400. One of the numbers is 134. What is the other number?   266

Children generally find subtraction more difficult than addition and it is important they recognize when each operation is best used. For example, it is possible to work out a "subtraction" problem by adding on ex. 17−9 could be thought of as "Add 1 to 9 to make 10, then add another 7 to make 17, so 1 and 7 have been added, making the answer 8." This is a perfectly legitimate method.

Answers:

22–23 Rounding Numbers
24–25 Lines of Symmetry

22 | **23**

① Amir has 48 football posters on his wall.
Rida has 33 pop group posters on her wall.

How many posters does Amir have to the nearest 10? **50**
How many posters does Rida have to the nearest 10? **30**

② A box has 49 raisins in it.

To the nearest 10, how many raisins would there be in three boxes? **150**

③ Marek and Mirka have a race to see who can run the farthest in two minutes.
Marek runs 530 yds and Mirka runs 670 yds.
How far does each child run to the nearest 100 yards?
Marek—500 yds   Mirka—700 yds

④ What is each amount to the nearest 10 ¢?
18 ¢ **20¢**   27 ¢ **30¢**   13 ¢ **10¢**   41 ¢ **40¢**   65 ¢ **70¢**

⑤ Igor collects Russian stamps and has 732.
Kira collects stamps from all over the world and has 4,600.

How many stamps does each child have to the nearest 1,000?
Igor—1,000 stamps   Kira—5,000 stamps

⑥ What is each length to the nearest 100 in?
82 in. **100 in.**   144 in. **100 in.**   370 in. **400 in.**   250 in. **300 in.**   190 in. **200 in.**

⑦ Most floorboards are about 87 in long.
About how long would three boards placed end to end be to the nearest 10 in? **270 in.**

⑧ What is each number to the nearest 1,000?
625 **1,000**   4,005 **4,000**   5,612 **6,000**   2,400 **2,000**   7,500 **8,000**

⑨ If Umi has 78 CDs and Tisa has twice as many, estimate to the nearest 10 how many CDs Tisa has. **160**

⑩ Diego can swim 6,500 yds without stopping.
Juanita can swim 4,800 yds without stopping.

How far can each swim to the nearest 1,000 yds?
Diego—7,000 yds   Juanita—5,000 yds

Rounding to the nearest 10, 100, or 1,000 is a very widely used skill and is very useful throughout life. In mathematics, as an international convention, the halfway point is usually rounded up so that 15, for example, would become 20 to the nearest 10 and 250 would become 300 to the nearest 100.

24 | **25**

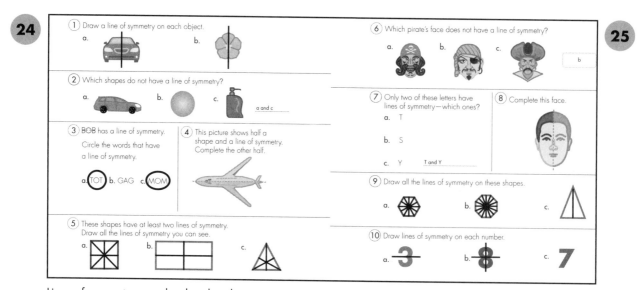

① Draw a line of symmetry on each object.
a.   b.

② Which shapes do not have a line of symmetry?
a.   b.   c.   a and c

③ BOB has a line of symmetry. Circle the words that have a line of symmetry.
a. TOT   b. GAG   c. MOM

④ This picture shows half a shape and a line of symmetry. Complete the other half.

⑤ These shapes have at least two lines of symmetry. Draw all the lines of symmetry you can see.
a.   b.   c.

⑥ Which pirate's face does not have a line of symmetry?
a.   b.   c.   b

⑦ Only two of these letters have lines of symmetry—which ones?
a. T
b. S
c. Y   T and Y

⑧ Complete this face.

⑨ Draw all the lines of symmetry on these shapes.
a.   b.   c.

⑩ Draw lines of symmetry on each number.
a. 3   b. 8   c. 7

Lines of symmetry are closely related to mirror images and just depend on a good eye for recognizing the symmetry if it exists. Symmetry of 2-D shapes can be trickier to spot as with the equilateral triangle which has three lines of symmetry. Your child will need to be careful with symmetry of some capital letters such as S and N, which do not have lines of symmetry.

Answers:

26–27 Multiplication Tables
28–29 3-D Shapes

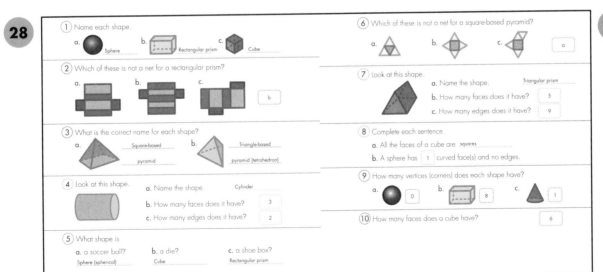

26

1. Carlo has saved 12 nickels. Bella has saved eight nickels. Each nickel is 5¢.
   How much money does each child have and who has the most?
   Carlo—60¢   Bella—40¢   Carlo has 20¢ more.

2. An octopus has eight legs. How many legs does each group have?
   16   32   24

3. Darius has two math classes each day.
   How many math classes will he have in
   5 days? 10   7 days? 14   9 days? 18   11 days? 22

4. Baseball cards come in packs of six.
   How many packs would Salim need to buy to have
   30 cards? 5   18 cards? 3   48 cards? 8   72 cards? 12

5. Marcel puts his comics in piles of three and has 12 piles.
   Chantal puts her comics in piles of four and has 11 piles.
   Which child has the most comics and by how many?
   Marcel—36   Chantal—44   Chantal by 8

27

6. Answer each question.
   $2 \times 3 =$ 6
   $3 \times 4 =$ 12
   $4 \times 5 =$ 20
   $5 \times 6 =$ 30
   $6 \times 8 =$ 48

7. Otto mixes pink paint by mixing three white cans with one red can.
   How many white cans will Otto need if he has seven red cans? 21
   How many white cans will Otto need if he has four red cans? 12
   How many red cans will Otto need if he has 12 white cans? 4

8. Ursula saves 5 dollars each week.
   How many dollars will she have after
   four weeks? 20   seven weeks? 35   10 weeks? 50   12 weeks? 60

9. How many eights are the same as
   16? 2   24? 3   40? 5   56? 7   88? 11

10. Answer each question.
    8 ×3 = 24   10 ×6 = 60   4 ×5 = 20   11 ×4 = 44   6 ×2 = 12

These questions are related to knowledge of times tables and ability to quickly and accurately recall times tables to solve simple problems. The wording of questions can sometimes confuse children but that is what happens in real life, and children need to become used to some questions being a little awkward.

28

1. Name each shape.
   a. Sphere   b. Rectangular prism   c. Cube

2. Which of these is not a net for a rectangular prism?
   a.   b.   c.   b

3. What is the correct name for each shape?
   a. Square-based pyramid   b. Triangle-based pyramid (tetrahedron)

4. Look at this shape.
   a. Name the shape. Cylinder
   b. How many faces does it have? 3
   c. How many edges does it have? 2

5. What shape is
   a. a soccer ball? Sphere (spherical)
   b. a die? Cube
   c. a shoe box? Rectangular prism

29

6. Which of these is not a net for a square-based pyramid?
   a.   b.   c.   a

7. Look at this shape.
   a. Name the shape. Triangular prism
   b. How many faces does it have? 5
   c. How many edges does it have? 9

8. Complete each sentence.
   a. All the faces of a cube are squares
   b. A sphere has 1 curved face(s) and no edges.

9. How many vertices (corners) does each shape have?
   a. 0   b. 8   c. 1

10. How many faces does a cube have? 6

Naming simple 3-D shapes is an important skill and continues to be so as the child gains an understanding of attributes such as faces, edges, and vertices. Nets for shapes can be awkward and some of the more complicated ones need imagination when seen on paper. It is helpful if you and your child actually make nets using pieces of paper or cardstock or cardboard.

Answers:

30–31 Multiplication
32–33 Charts and Tables

30

1. In a race, Robert cycles 275 yds. Becky cycles twice as far.
   How far does Becky cycle?
   550 yds

2. What is 48 multiplied by three? 144

3. A car travels 270 miles in a day.
   If the car travels the same distance for three days, how far will it have gone? 810 miles

4. Work out each multiplication problem.

   a. $\begin{array}{r} 72 \\ \times\ 3 \\ \hline 216 \end{array}$ b. $\begin{array}{r} 140 \\ \times\ 4 \\ \hline 560 \end{array}$ c. $\begin{array}{r} 195 \\ \times\ 2 \\ \hline 390 \end{array}$

5. A gardener grows 16 cabbages in each row.
   If the gardener plants six rows, how many cabbages will grow?
   96

31

6. Work out each multiplication problem.

   a. $\begin{array}{r} 50 \\ \times\ 4 \\ \hline 200 \end{array}$ b. $\begin{array}{r} 75 \\ \times\ 3 \\ \hline 225 \end{array}$ c. $\begin{array}{r} 150 \\ \times\ 4 \\ \hline 600 \end{array}$

7. Wendy saves 45 ¢ each week for six weeks.
   How much will Wendy have saved after six weeks? 270¢ ($2.70)

8. Shen has downloaded 53 tracks to his mp3 player.
   Zan has downloaded three times as many.
   How many tracks has Zan downloaded? 159

9. Work out each multiplication problem.

   a. $\begin{array}{r} 20 \\ \times\ 4 \\ \hline 80 \end{array}$ b. $\begin{array}{r} 40 \\ \times\ 5 \\ \hline 200 \end{array}$ c. $\begin{array}{r} 60 \\ \times\ 6 \\ \hline 360 \end{array}$

10. How much more is nine times ten than nine times nine?
    9

Multiplication problems come in many forms and your child needs to recognize when multiplying is the best option. As has always been the case, a very good knowledge of times tables is critical for success to be achieved here. Not just accurate recall but also speedy recall is important.

32

1. A child kept a record of the birds she saw in her backyard in one week.
   Look at this chart and then answer the questions.

Owls	🦉🦉
Robins	🐦🐦🐦🐦🐦
Sparrows	🐦🐦🐦🐦🐦🐦🐦🐦🐦
Starlings	🐦🐦
Swallows	🐦

   a. Which bird did she see the most? How many did she see?
      Sparrow—9 times

   b. How many more sparrows did she see than robins? 4

   c. How many birds did she see altogether? 19

   d. Which birds did she see only twice?
      Owls and starlings

33

2. Four children were asked to complete this table about their favorite activities.
   Look carefully at this table and then answer the questions.

Name	Music	Sport	Class
Katie	Pop	Jogging	English
David	Jazz	Hockey	Math
Clara	Disco	Gymnastics	Math
Oliver	Pop	Trampoline	Phys Ed

   a. Who said hockey was their favorite sport? David

   b. Who had disco as their favorite music? Clara

   c. Did any of the children enjoy French class? No

   d. How many different types of music are on the table? 3

   e. Did Clara and Oliver share any favorites? No

3. Complete the same table for a few of your family or friends.

Name	Music	Sport	Lesson
	Answers will vary.	Answers will vary.	Answers will vary.
	Answers will vary.	Answers will vary.	Answers will vary.
	Answers will vary.	Answers will vary.	Answers will vary.
	Answers will vary.	Answers will vary.	Answers will vary.

   Write three of your own questions about your table.
   a. Questions will vary.
   b. Questions will vary.
   c. Questions will vary.

Children usually find tables and charts interesting and fairly easy to deal with. It is vital to read data carefully. In question 3, encourage your child to think up some good questions.

Answers:

34–35 Patterns
36–37 Division

34

① Complete this pattern.

② Continue this sequence.

123, 1234, 12345, `123456` `1234567`

③ Continue this pattern.

④ What comes next?

⑤ Fill in the missing numbers.

a. 0 `2` 4 `6` 8 10

b. `5` 7 9 `11` 13

35

⑥ Continue this pattern.

⑦ Fill in the missing numbers.

a. 3 6 9 12 15 18 21 24

b. 25 30 35 40 45 50 55

⑧ What comes next?

1,3   2,6   3,9   `4,12`   `5,15`

⑨ Fill in the missing numbers.

a. 49, 42, `35` 28, `21` 14

b. 63, 54, `45` `36` 27

⑩ What comes next?

Continuing and completing patterns is very much the same concept as sequencing. It relies on your child's ability to spot what is happening in the given pattern or number sequence and then continuing the same sequence correctly.

36

① A pizza is cut into eight slices. Four children share the pizza.
How many pieces does each child receive? `2`

② 30 bananas are shared equally between five monkeys.
How many bananas will each monkey receive? `6`

③ Answer each question.
a. What is 14 divided by 2? `7`
b. What is 20 divided by 5? `4`
c. 16 shared by 2 is `8`
d. 30 shared by 3 is `10`

④ A number divided by 2 is 9.
What is the number? `18`

⑤ Answer each question.
a. 12 ÷ 2 = `6`   b. 15 ÷ 3 = `5`
c. 20 ÷ 4 = `5`   d. 25 ÷ 5 = `5`

37

⑥ A farmer gives four hay bales to veach cow.
If the farmer gives out 40 hay bales, how many cows does he have? `10`

⑦ Dave collects 5¢ coins and has saved 50¢.
How many 5¢ coins has Dave collected? `10`

⑧ Answer each question.
a. What is 35 divided by 5? `7`
b. What is 32 shared by 4? `8`
c. Divide 21 by 3. `7`
d. Divide 45 by 5. `9`

⑨ Choc Chub candies are put into packs of five.
a. How many packs will be needed for 85 Choc Chubs? `17`
b. How many packs will be needed for 200 Choc Chubs? `40`

⑩ Four runners run in a relay race. They each cover an equal distance. The race is 600yds.
How far does each runner run? `150yds`

Younger children will be made aware of the idea of sharing and sharing equally. As your child grows, ideas of dividing and division are introduced and various methods of dealing with division problems are taught. At this stage, division is very much the reverse of multiplication and as such, knowledge of times tables is once again critical for success.

73

Answers:

38–39 Telling Time
42–43 Fractions

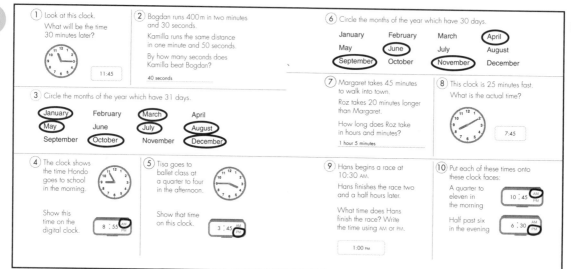

When writing times onto digital clocks make sure that your child has included AM or PM to distinguish between before-noon and after-noon times. Look at a variety of digital clock faces with your child to gain a good understanding of the basics as the markings can be even more diverse.

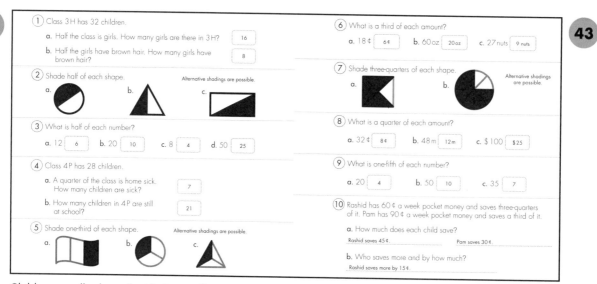

Children usually do well with the smaller unitary fractions such as ½, ⅓, and ¼ but once again, true proficiency will be greatly aided by very good knowledge of times tables. The child should understand that numbers can be broken down into parts smaller than 1. Fractions are one method to write a number smaller than one, and decimals are another.

Answers:

44–45 Measuring Volume
46–47 Money Challenge

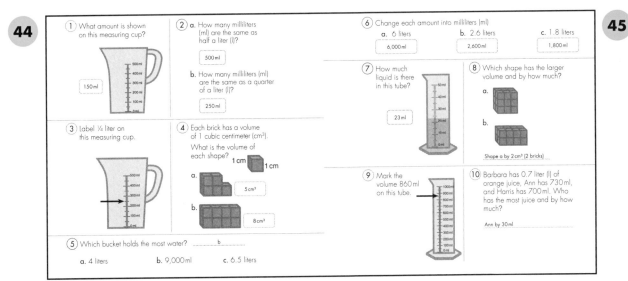

44

① What amount is shown on this measuring cup?

150 ml

② a. How many milliliters (ml) are the same as half a liter (l)?

500 ml

b. How many milliliters (ml) are the same as a quarter of a liter (l)?

250 ml

③ Label ¼ liter on this measuring cup.

④ Each brick has a volume of 1 cubic centimeter (cm³). What is the volume of each shape?

a. 5 cm³

b. 8 cm³

⑤ Which bucket holds the most water?   b

a. 4 liters   b. 9,000 ml   c. 6.5 liters

45

⑥ Change each amount into milliliters (ml)

a. 6 liters — 6,000 ml
b. 2.6 liters — 2,600 ml
c. 1.8 liters — 1,800 ml

⑦ How much liquid is there in this tube?

23 ml

⑧ Which shape has the larger volume and by how much?

a.

b.

Shape a by 2 cm³ (2 bricks)

⑨ Mark the volume 860 ml on this tube.

⑩ Barbara has 0.7 liter (l) of orange juice, Ann has 730 ml, and Harris has 700 ml. Who has the most juice and by how much?

Ann by 30 ml

Knowing the relationship between units is important. Here your child needs to know that 1,000 ml = 1 liter. For the younger child, the number 1,000 can be daunting so lots of practical help with measuring volumes should be given. As with other exercises of this type, lots of different devices for measuring and scale types exist. The more your child can be shown the better!

46

① Write these amounts as dollars and cents.

a. 452¢ — $4.52
b. 1,270¢ — $12.70
c. 3,285¢ — $32.85

② Darius has three coins and they add up to 35¢.

What are the three coins?   25¢ + 5¢ + 5¢

③ Patrice has these coins in his hand but needs one dollar.

How much more does Patrice need?   9¢

④ Write these amounts as cents only.

a. $2.36 — 236¢
b. $7.42 — 742¢
c. $42.75 — 4,275¢

⑤ Bonnie earns 50¢ every time she cleans her mother's car. How much will Bonnie earn if she cleans the car…

a. twice? — $1.00
b. 5 times? — $2.50
c. 10 times? — $5.00

47

⑥ a. How many 25¢ have the same value as $1.00?   4
b. How many 5¢ have the same value as $1.00?   20
c. How many 10¢ have the same value as $2.00?   20

⑦ Work out each sum.

a. 17¢
   + 14¢
   ____
    31¢

b. 26¢
   + 38¢
   ____
    64¢

c. 54¢
   + 36¢
   ____
    90¢

⑧ Kareem has three 10¢ and two 5¢. Salima has two 10¢, three 5¢, and four 1¢.

a. How much does each child have?

Kareem — 40¢   Salim — 39¢

b. Who has the most and by how much?   Kareem by 1¢

⑨ Solve the difference.

a. 40¢
   − 18¢
   ____
    22¢

b. 53¢
   − 47¢
   ____
     6¢

c. 27¢
   − 19¢
   ____
     8¢

⑩ Bella has four coins in her hand. The value of Bella's coins is 41¢. Which coins does Bella have?   25¢ + 10¢ + 5¢ + 1¢

Having children work with coins and money is a very valuable way of helping them to understand numbers. Some families have a jar or pot where spare coins are kept and this can be used to create a few simple problems here and there. These questions help to reinforce what has been taught at school.

Answers:

48–49 Angle Turns
50–51 Problem Solving

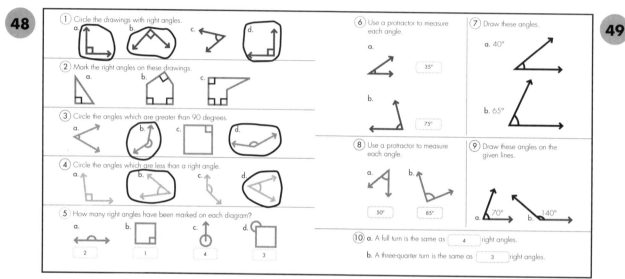

Children should know that an angle is formed by two rays (sides) that share a common endpoint (vertex). The angle is the amount of turn, measured in degrees. Explain with a door opening and closing. If your child is struggling, talk about the door opening a little—a small angle—or a lot—a larger angle. The right angle is a special case and an important one. Children are often given practice in drawing and measuring angles.

These questions are for general practice. Irrespective of whether children get a question right or wrong, it is important to sometimes ask how they did it. Some children develop their own weird and wonderful ways of answering problems, which can be fast and accurate. Others pick up odd ideas that may be right sometimes or may be slow and ineffective at other times.

Answers:

52–53 Diagrams
54–55 Probability Problems

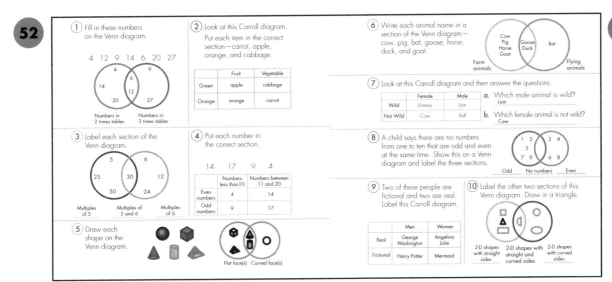

Venn and Carroll diagrams are not as popular in the math classroom as they once were but are still very valid and useful means of handling data. Children usually pick up the basic ideas very quickly but the more practice the better. Carroll diagrams are named after their originator Lewis Carroll, the author of Alice in Wonderland. Carroll's real name was Charles Dodgson and in that guise he was a mathematician.

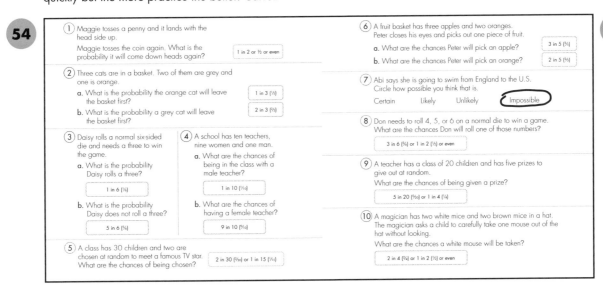

At this stage children are only expected to have a fairly simple understanding of probability and with the use of a die or a coin a lot of ground can be covered. The ideas of "likely," "unlikely," "certain," "even," and "impossible" are tricky for youngsters and so fun and interesting examples should be used.

78

Answers:

56–57 Measuring Speed
58–59 Tables and Charts

56

1. Jacek walks 3 miles in one hour. Victoria walks 4 miles in two hours.
If they continue walking at the same speed, how far will they each
walk in 6 hours?
Jacek — 18 miles   Victoria — 12 miles

2. Krysta cycles 0.2 miles in 3 minutes.
   a. If Krysta cycles at the same speed, how
   long will it take her to cycle 1 mile?   15 minutes
   b. What speed is Krysta cycling in miles
   per hour?   4 miles per hour (mph)

3. Marcel swims 1,200 yds in half an hour.
Angelique swims 500 yds in 15 minutes.
After one hour, who has swam the farthest and by what distance?
Marcel — 2,400 yds   Angelique — 2,000 yds   Marcel by 400 yds

4. A car travels at 60 mph for one hour.
How far does it travel every ten minutes?
10 miles

5. A tortoise can travel 8 in in ten minutes.
If the tortoise keeps the same speed,
how far will it travel in two hours?
96 in

57

6. Billy drives his car at the same speed for three hours.
In three hours, Billy travels 180 miles.
What is Billy's speed?   60 mph

7. A train can go from New York City to Trenton in
60 minutes. The distance for the train is 60 miles.
A car travels the same distance but in 90 minutes.
What is the speed of the car?   40 mph

8. Daisy jogs a distance of 2 miles in 20 minutes.
   a. If Daisy jogs at the same speed all the time,
   how far can she jog in one hour?   6 miles
   b. How far does Daisy jog in one minute?   0.1 miles

9. Which is fastest?
   a. 200 yds traveled in 5 minutes.
   b. 300 yds traveled in 15 minutes.   a
   c. 400 yds traveled in 20 minutes.

10. Katie's bus travels at a steady speed of 60 miles per hour.
The bus travels 240 miles. How long has Katie been traveling?
4 hours

The concept of speed can be difficult for a child but reference to speeds of cars or relative speeds of snails over horses can help to exemplify various speeds.

58

Tommy collects information about the different types of birds in his garden. He collects the data using a tally chart. These are his results.

Birds	Tallies
Sparrow	卌 卌 卌 卌 卌 IIII
Robin	卌 III
Hummingbird	I
Cardinal	IIII
Blue Jay	卌 卌 卌 II
Pigeon	卌 卌 卌 III

1. a. How many robins did Tommy see?   8
   b. How many pigeons did Tommy see?   18

2. a. Which bird did Tommy see the most?   Sparrow
   b. Which bird did Tommy see the least?   Hummingbird

3. How many birds did Tommy see in total?   82

4. How many more sparrows did Tommy see than blue jays?   7

5. How many types of bird did Tommy see less than ten times?   3

59

A group of friends make a chart of their classmates' favorite sports. Each child could choose just one sport.
These are the results.

6. a. Which was the favorite sport?   Swimming
   b. Which was the least favorite sport?   Soccer

7. How many more children preferred baseball to tennis?   1

8. How many children were there in the class?   32

9. Which two sports together had a total vote of 7?
Soccer and Hockey

10. Put a label on each axis.

Reading information from tables and charts is an important skill. It is also important for children to create their own tables and charts and then write good questions to go with them.